Hey Kids! Let's Visit Rome Italy

Fun, Facts, and Amazing Discoveries for Kids

Teresa Mills

Life Experiences Publishing

Contents

Welcome

Rome is one of Italy's most important cities and a major tourist destination. The eternal city has a fascinating and splendid past, as well as some of the most stunning architecture in the world. Rome is an incredible place to visit – from the ruins of the ancient city to awe-inspiring cathedrals and churches, from world-class art museums to contemporary arts and fashion shows, from fine-dining establishments to local trattorias, from the Vatican museums to the Spanish Steps – Rome has it all.

This book is written as a fun fact guide about some attractions and sites in Rome. It includes some history interspersed with fun facts about things to do. The book can easily be enjoyed by younger children through reading it with them. You can visit Rome right from your own home! Whether you are preparing for a vacation with the family and want to learn more about the city or just enjoying the pictures to learn a little more about Rome, this book is for you.

As you continue to learn more about Rome, I have some fun activity pages that you can download and print:

https://kid-friendly-family-vacations.com/romefun

When you have completed this book, I invite you to enjoy the other books in the series. We visit Washington DC, a Cruise Ship, New York City, London England, San Francisco, Savannah Georgia, Paris France, Charleston South Carolina, Chicago, Boston, Philadelphia, San Diego, Seattle, Seoul South Korea, Atlanta, and Dublin Ireland!

Enjoy!

Teresa Mills

A Little About Rome

Rome is a city full of history – almost 3000 years of history! It is the capital city of Italy with a population of more than 2.8 million, making it a very busy modern city. That is one of the most fascinating things to me about walking around Rome. One minute you are walking down a road filled with busy modern-day businesspeople and cars, and the next minute you are standing in front of the ancient Roman Colosseum – crazy!

Legend has it that Rome was founded in 753 BC by the twins Romulus and Remus. This theory is from an ancient roman myth. The myth explains that Romulus and Remus decided to build a city, then after an argument, Romulus killed Remus and the city was named Rome for Romulus.

Rome plays a major role in the Roman Catholic Church, as it is the home to the mini state of Vatican City. The pope is the leader of Vatican City, which incorporates the Vatican Museums, St. Peter's Basilica, and the Sistine Chapel.

Rome is basically one big museum. There is so much history to see – literally around every corner.

So kids... Let's Visit Rome Italy!

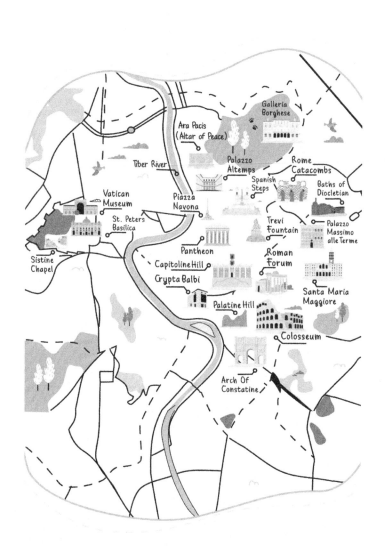

Galleria
Borghese

Ara Pacis
(Altar of Peace)

Tiber River

Palazzo
Altemps

Rome
Catacombs

Spanish
Steps

Baths of
Diocletian

Vatican
Museum

Piazza
Navona

St. Peters
Basilica

Trevi
Fountain

Palazzo
Massimo
alle Terme

Sistine
Chapel

Pantheon

Capitoline Hill

Crypta Balbi

Roman
Forum

Santa Maria
Maggiore

Palatine Hill

Colosseum

Arch Of
Constatine

Chapter 1

The Pantheon

The Pantheon in Rome is one of the most well-preserved ancient Roman monuments in the world! It is a perfect example of Roman architecture as its magnificent concrete dome is virtually intact after almost 2000 years. The dome is a perfect hemisphere, and the oculus in the center of the top of the dome provides natural light to the building.

The portico of the Pantheon is made up of sixteen columns made with Egyptian granite. The columns are 39 feet tall and weigh close to 60 tons each. The decorative tops of the columns are carved from white Greek granite. The columns were made in Egypt and "shipped" from there. This shipping involved dragging the columns from the quarry to the river, floating down the Nile River, and then being transferred to vessels to cross the Mediterranean Sea to Ostia. From Ostia, the columns were moved back to barges and floated up the Tiber River to Rome.

The interior of the Pantheon is a large room covered by the dome. The oculus is not covered so rain will fall into the building. The floor is built at a 30-degree angle and is equipped with drains to handle the runoff.

The Pantheon

The name Pantheon means "relating to or common to all gods." Breaking the Ancient Greek word *pantheon* apart, *pan* means "all" and *theon* (theos) means "of or sacred to a god." The simplest explanation for the name of the Pantheon seems to be that it was dedicated to all the gods.

The Pantheon was formerly a Roman temple and later a Catholic church. It is in use as a Catholic church to this day. In addition to being an operating church, the Pantheon is the burial place for two kings of Italy (Vittorio Emanuele II and Umberto I), Umberto's Queen (Margherita), painters (Raphael and Annibale Carracci), the composer Arcangelo Corelli, and architect Baldassare Peruzzi to name a few.

Fun Facts about the Pantheon

- The current Pantheon is the third version after the first two burned down in fires.

- The oculus, which is the opening of the dome and the source of light for the Pantheon, is 30 Roman feet (approximately 9 meters / 29.13 feet) in diameter.

- The rotunda of the Pantheon is a perfect hemisphere, which measures from the inner circle 43.3 meters / 142 feet in diameter (the exact height of the dome from the floor to the oculus).

Chapter 2

The Colosseum

The Roman Colosseum is an oval amphitheater located in the city center of Rome. Construction of the colosseum began in 72 AD under emperor Vespasian and was completed in 80 AD under emperor Titus. At the time of its construction, the colosseum was known as the Flavian Amphitheater (both emperor Vespasian and Titus were a part of the Flavian Dynasty).

The huge structure was approximately 189 by 156 meters (620 by 513 feet) and stood over 4 stories tall. The amphitheater had 80 entrances – 76 for visitors, 2 for event participants, and 2 exclusively for the emperor. This large amphitheater could seat more than 50,000 guests. At the opening of the colosseum, emperor Titus held 100 days of gladiatorial games. Gladiatorial games included gladiators fighting animals (bears, rhinos, tigers, elephants, and giraffes), or animals fighting animals. There were also chariot races, processions, and mock naval battles.

The Roman Colosseum

The interior of the colosseum is an intricate array of tunnels and passageways and an underground staging area for the games. Modern architects are learning more and more about the structure under the arena floor. Many believe that workmen under the arena floor could use a winch attached to the wall along with other tools to raise and lower animal cages directly into the arena. The staging area was used to hold animals, slaves, prisoners, and gladiators before their performances. The underground staging area is called the hypogeum.

The plumbing system under the arena also allowed the entire arena to be flooded to simulate the ocean for naval battle preparation.

Passageways under the arena floor

Fun Facts about the Colosseum

- Gladiators who fought in the colosseum were essentially slaves. Being a gladiator was not really a choice but a necessity for survival.

- The colosseum is one of the seven wonders of the world. It was given this designation in 2007.

- The colosseum is the world's largest amphitheater.

Chapter 3

Capitoline Hill

Capitoline Hill is located close to the Roman Forum, the Colosseum, and Palatine Hill. It is considered the most important of the seven hills of Rome, and it is also the smallest of the hills. This hill symbolizes the epicenter of the Roman Empire and contains the most important temples of the city. Capitoline Hill is the religious and political heart of Rome.

History says that Capitoline Hill was chosen by Romulus to be the starting point of the city of Rome. Capitoline Hill houses several important temples: the temple of Juno Monets, the temple of Virtus, and the temple of Jupiter Optimus Maximus Capitolinus. The temple of Jupiter is almost as large as the Parthenon (in Greece) and is the most important of these temples as Capitoline Hill and Jupiter became symbols of Rome.

Architect and Renaissance artist Michelangelo Buonarroti created the current design of the Piazza del

Campidoglio (the square at the top of Capitoline Hill). His designs for the piazza date between 1536 and 1546. The new design was commissioned to impress Charles V (Holy Roman Emperor of Austria from 1519 to 1556) who would be visiting Rome in 1538. This visit gave Michelangelo the opportunity to build a civic plaza that was monumental for Rome to reestablish its grandeur. The piazza is framed by three palaces: the Palazzo Senatorio in the center, the Palazzo dei Conservatori on the south side, and the Palazzo Nuovo, on the north side.

In the center of the piazza stands the equestrian statue of Emperor Marcus Aurelius, who was emperor of Rome from 161 to 180 AD. The bronze status that stands in the piazza today is a copy. The original statue of Marcus Aurelius can be found in the Palazzo dei Conservatori.

Capitoline Hill

Fun Facts about Capitoline Hill

- Capitoline Hill began as the starting point of Romulus's Rome and has been transformed into one of the busiest and most beautiful piazzas in Rome.

- Before the 1536 renovation of Capitoline Hill, the area had become a meadow of weeds and was used for grazing animals.

- In ancient times, Capitoline Hill was an important religious area.

Chapter 4

Santa Maria Maggiore

The Basilica di Santa Maria Maggiore (Basilica of Saint Mary Major) is a major (or papal) basilica in the Roman Catholic church. Located atop Esquiline Hill, it is one of only four major basilicas which are all a part of the Diocese of Rome. The other three major basilicas in the Roman Diocese are: St. Peter's Basilica, St. John Lateran, and St. Paul Outside the Walls.

Santa Maria Maggiore was one of the first churches built to honor the Virgin Mary. It was built after the Council of Ephesus of 431 (a council of Christian bishops which met in Ephesus to come to consensus for all of Christendom), which proclaimed Mary as the mother of God. Mosaics in the nave and triumphal arch depict the life of Mary and the life of Christ. There are also scenes from the Old Testament of the Bible including Moses and the Red Sea. The basilica is the largest and oldest of at least 26 churches in Rome built to honor the Virgin Mary.

The Crypt of Nativity (Bethlehem Crypt) is under the high alter of the basilica. It contains a crystal reliquary (a container for holy relics) which is said to contain wood from the Holy Crib of the nativity of Jesus Christ. The bell tower sits at 75 meters (246 feet) tall and dates back to 1375-1376. The tower is built in the Roman style and has five bells.

Basilica di Santa Maria Maggiore

Fun Facts about Santa Maria Maggiore

- At 75 meters (246 feet), the medieval bell tower atop Santa Maria Maggiore is the tallest in Rome.

- Santa Maria Maggiore still maintains its beautiful structure, built in the 5th century.

- As Santa Maria Maggiore is a papal basilica, it is visited frequently by the pope. The pope assigns an archpriest (usually a cardinal) to be in charge of the basilica on a day-to-day basis.

Chapter 5

Palatine Hill

Palatine Hill is one of the most ancient parts of Rome and is the most centrally located of the seven hills of the city. Today, it is essentially an open-air museum called the Palatine Museum. Palatine Hill is located about 40 meters (131 feet) above the Roman Forum.

Excavations done in Palatine during the 1900s show that people lived in this area as far back as the 10th century BC. Excavations continued and uncovered Palatine House in 2006. Palatine House is believed to be the birthplace of Augustus – Rome's first emperor. It was a two-story house deemed to be a very "aristocratic house" built around an atrium. Livia, the wife of Augustus, also had a home on Palatine Hill. Her home was better preserved and features a reception hall and a square atrium. Her home contained notable paintings that were fairly well preserved.

Palatine Hill - House of Livia Augustus

Among the ruins on Palatine Hill are Domitian's Palace and Hippodrome. This is one of the largest complexes on Palatine Hill. The palace stretches across most of Palatine Hill with barrel vaults and arched walls. Hippodrome was a part of the palace though its use is not completely known. Some think that maybe it was a gymnasium, training ground, or just a part of the gardens.

Palatine Hill also features imperial palaces, the cryptoporticus (a 130-meter / 427 feet long passageway between places), Farnese Gardens (the first botanical garden in Europe), and the Palatine Museum (a museum displaying fragments of large sculptures found during the excavation).

Palatine Hill - Domitian's Hippodrome

Fun Facts about Palatine Hill

- The word "Palatine" is the origin of the word "palace.. The words "palazzo" in Italian and "palais" in French are also derived from the word "Palatine."

- Palatine Hill offers the best views of Rome. In fact, it's the only place in the center of Rome where you have great views of the Circus Maximus, the Colosseum, and the whole Roman Forum.

- The hut of Romulus and his twin brother Remus was on Palatine Hill. Legend has it, and excavations back this up, that the rise of Rome as a military power began on this hill.

Chapter 6

The Roman Forum

The history of the Roman Forum stretches back to the time before the birth of Christ. Many historians have estimated that public events first took place in the Forum around 500 BC at the time of the Roman Republic. As the use of the Forum increased, arches, statues, basilicas, and other buildings were constructed. This continued up until the reign of Julius Caesar (dictator of Rome from 49 BC-44 BC), when the Forum was becoming overcrowded. Julius Caesar is credited with the construction of a new forum to the side of the original.

Situated between Palatine Hill and Capitoline Hill, the Roman Forum was historically considered one of the most celebrated meeting places in the world. Originally a marketplace, today the Roman Forum is a rectangular plaza that is surrounded by the ruins of some important ancient government buildings in the center of the city. For many years, it was the center of daily life for the citizens of Rome. The Forum provided a place for elections, public speeches, trials, and even gladiatorial matches in 509 BC-27 BC before the colosseum was built.

The Roman Forum

After the fall of the Roman Empire (27 BC-476 AD), the Roman Forum was all but forgotten and eventually buried underground. It was not until the 20th century that excavations began taking place to uncover the Roman Forum.

Some of the notable structures in the Forum are:

The Senate House (The Curia Julia) - The senate met here to make governmental decisions about Rome. It was converted to a church in 630 AD.

Temple of Saturn - The ruins of this temple date back to about 42 BC. This temple was dedicated to Saturn, the god of agriculture.

Arch or Titus - Built after the death or emperor Titus, it is a triumphal arch symbolizing Rome's victory over Jerusalem.

Temple of Vesta - It was constructed around 81 AD by emperor Domitian to honor his brother emperor Titus. Titus was victorious in the siege of Jerusalem.

Arch of Septimius Severus - Erected in 203 AD, this arch commemorated the 3rd anniversary of emperor Septimius Severus.

Temple of Antonius and Faustina - This best-preserved temple in the Forum was built in the 2nd century.

Basilica of Maxentius - The size of the ruins of this basilica suggest that it was one of the most important buildings in the Roman Forum.

Column of Phocas – This column was erected in 608 AD in honor of emperor Byzantium. It is one of the few constructions that have remained standing since being built.

Via Sacra – This main road in ancient Rome linked the Plaza of Capitoline Hill to the Colosseum.

Fun Facts about the Roman Forum

- The treasury at the time was kept in the Temple of Saturn.

- Severed heads of defeated public enemies used to be displayed on the platform where magistrates and speakers would address the people of Rome. Cicero met this fate and had his head displayed by Mark Anthony in 43 BC.

- One of the world's earliest sewer systems allowed the building of the Forum. The Cloaca Maxima sewer was built around 600 BC to help drain the area between Palatine and Capitoline Hills.

Chapter 7

Arch of Constantine

Located between the Colosseum and Palatine Hill, the Arch of Constantine is a triumphal arch. It was erected 312 AD to commemorate Constantine's (Constantine the Great - Roman emperor form 306 AD-337 AD) victory at the Battle of Milvian Bridge over Maxentius (a Roman emperor from 306 AD-312 AD – he was recognized by the Roman Senate as emperor but not by his fellow emperors).

Did you notice that the years of ruling as emperors for Constantine and Maxentius overlapped? During this time in history, the Roman Empire was governed by a Tetrarch system, which is where four people jointly govern. This system divided the empire between two senior emperors (the augusti) and their juniors (the caesars). The caesars would succeed the region's emperor upon their death or retirement. The Roman Empire was divided into the Eastern Empire with a capitol in Byzantium (Constantinople, now Istanbul) and the Western Empire with a capitol in Milan. Rome was the ceremonial capitol of the Roman Empire.

The Arch of Constantine

The significance of the Arch of Constantine was not only to commemorate Constantine's political transformation of Rome but also the tolerance of Christianity in the Roman Empire. Constantine the Great was the first Roman Emperor to convert to Christianity, and he lived out that belief by helping to influence the Edict of Milan in 313 AD, which was an agreement to treat Christians nicely within the Roman Empire.

Fun Facts about the Arch of Constantine

- Constantine was an important part of the rise of Christianity in Europe.

- The Arch of Constantine is the largest triumphal arch remaining in Rome.

- The arch is 21 meters (69 feet) high, 25.9 meters (85 feet) wide and 7.4 meters (24.3 feet) deep.

- The ends of the Arch of Constantine are decorated. This is not always the case with triumphal monuments.

Chapter 8

Galleria Borghese

Housed in the former Villa Borghese Pinciana, the Galleria Borghese (Borghese Gallery) is an art gallery in Rome. It contains a large private art collection of Cardinal Scipione Borghese. It's one of the largest private collections of sculptures, paintings, and antiquities in the world.

The architect Flaminio Ponzio designed the building that houses the gallery. Its construction began in 1612. After Ponzio passed away in 1613, the work was finished by Giovanni Vasanzio. The building underwent a redesign in 1775 under architect Antonio Asprucci. At that time, the antiques and sculptures were reordered according to themes. By the end of the 18th century, the gallery was transformed into a public museum.

After the Borghese family could no longer manage the maintenance costs, the collection was sold to the Italian

State. The building was restored again between 1995 and 1997.

The Galleria Borghese

Fun Facts about the Galleria Borghese

- The Galleria Borghese is located in the 3rd largest public park in Rome, the Villa Borghese Gardens.

- Admirable and great artworks include Apollo and Daphne by Bernini, Pauline Bonaparte as Venus Victrix, Canova, Boy with a Basket of Fruit, Caravaggio, Sacred and Profane Love by Titian, The Enchantress Circe (or Melissa) by Dosso Dossi etc.

- The little sister of Napoleon Bonaparte, Pauline, married a Borghese (Don Camillo Filippo Ludovico Borghese) in 1803. Due to being given several titles by Napoleon after the marriage, "Prince Camillo" agreed to sell some of the most famous sculptures in the collection. These works were then moved to the Louvre for display.

Chapter 9

Trevi Fountain

Measuring 49 meters (approximately 161 feet) wide and 26 meters (approximately 86 feet) tall, the beautiful Trevi Fountain can be found at the intersection of three streets (De Crocicchia St., Poli St., and Delle Muratte St.) in downtown Rome. The name Trevi actually derives from the Latin word trivium meaning "intersection of three streets." The fountain also marks the ending point of the modern aqueduct Acqua Vergine, one of the aqueducts that supplied ancient Rome with water.

Although the aqueducts and water supply for the fountain have been around since before Christ (19 BC), the construction of the fountain that we see today did not start until 1732. As early as 1629, Pope Urban VIII asked for sketches for a fountain to be drawn up, but that project was abandoned when the Pope passed away. In 1730, Pope Clement XII asked for designs again in the form of a contest. Architect Nicola Slavi lost the competition to Alessandro Galilei but was ultimately

awarded the commission due to a dispute among the
public over a Florentine winning the competition. Salvi
died before the fountain was constructed, so architect
Giuseppe Pannini was hired to complete the job.

The Trevi Fountain

The fountain has been renovated and restored several
times over the years: in 1988 (to remove smog
discoloration), 1998 (scrubbed and cracks repaired), and
2014-2015 (a 20-month restoration including 100 LED
lights).

One great tradition surrounding the Trevi Fountain has
to be mentioned here! Throwing a coin (or two or three)
into the fountain with your eyes closed using your right

hand to toss the coin backwards over your left shoulder is a must-do while in Rome. Legend has it that according to the number of coins you toss, something will come true:

- Toss one coin – you will return to Rome one day.

- Toss two coins – you will find true love in Rome.

- Toss three coins – you will marry the love you met in Rome.

So, when you visit Rome, will you toss a coin into the Trevi Fountain? Some toss a coin and make a wish.

Fun Facts about the Trevi Fountain

- It is estimated that over 3,000 euros are tossed into the fountain every day. Some years, the total tossed into the fountain is over 1.4 million euros (approximately 1.3 million dollars). The money collected from the fountain is donated to charities in Rome.

- The Trevi Fountain has appeared in several movies including *The Lizzie McGuire Movie* in 2003.

- The fountain is replicated at Walt Disney World's EPCOT.

Chapter 10

Piazza Navona

Piazza Navona is a public square in Rome and is the home to three fountains. The piazza is a lively place during the day as it is surrounded by terraces and restaurants. On many days, you will see street entertainers performing here. During the Christmas season, the market is transformed into a large Christmas market.

The piazza is located on the former location of the Stadium of Domitian, which was founded in 86 AD. It was paved over in the 15th century and a city market was hosted there for almost 300 years. Built in 1651 by Gian Lorenzo Bernini, the Fontana dei Quattro (Fountain of the Four Rivers) is the center piece of the piazza. At the south end of the piazza is another fountain, the Fontana del Moro by Giacomo della Porta built in 1575 and on the north end is the Fountain of Neptune built in 1574 by the same architect.

Piazza Navona

Fun Facts about Piazza Navona

- Up until the mid-19th century, the drains of the three fountains were blocked during the summer and the center was flooded to create the "Lake of Piazza Navona."

- The fountain is featured in many films including Dan Brown's *Angels & Demons, National Lampoon's European Vacation,* and *American Assassin.*

- Sant'Agnese in Agone Church, located at the edge of the center of Piazza Navona, is dedicated to a young girl named Agnese who was killed there because she did not wish to date and devoted herself to Christianity.

Chapter 11

Spanish Steps

The Spanish Steps are a steep 135-step staircase that leads from the Piazza di Spagna up to the Piazza Trinita dei Monti and the Trinita dei Monte church. The steps were built by architects Francesco de Sanctis and Alessandro Specchi in the years 1723-1725. The three tiers of the steps are dedicated to the Holy Trinity (the Father, Son, and Holy Ghost). Once built, the staircase made the area of Piazza di Spagna a very popular area to live.

Once upon a time, it was a great pastime for locals and iconic for tourists to sit on the steps. But as of August 2019, for additional security in downtown Rome you are no longer allowed to sit on the steps. Sitting on the steps will now cost you a fine of at least 400 euros (approximately $392).

The Spanish Steps

The iconic Spanish Steps have been very popular in movies and TV. You will see the Spanish Steps in *Roman Holiday* (1953), *The Girl Who Knew Too Much* (1963), *The Roman Spring of Mrs. Stone* (1961), *The Talented Mr. Ripley* (1999), *Everybody Loves Raymond* (Season 5, Episode 1 2000), *Gunslinger Girl* (Episode 6-Gelato 2007), *To Rome With Love* (2012), *The Amazing Race 24* (2014), *The Man from U.N.C.L.E.* (2015), and likely many more.

Fun Facts about The Spanish Steps

- The English poet John Keats lived and died in 1821 in a house at the corner on the right as you start up the steps. The house is now a museum.

- On June 13, 2007, a drunk driver attempted to drive his Toyota Celica down the Spanish Steps. Several of the 200-year-old steps were chipped and scuffed, but no one was hurt. The driver was arrested.

- The first McDonalds restaurant in Italy was opened near the Spanish Steps on March 20, 1986.

Chapter 12

Catacombs of Rome

The Catacombs of Rome are subterranean (underground) burial places in and around Rome. Catacombs were mostly famous for Christian burials and there are at least 40 throughout the Rome area. Other religions, including the Jews and some pagan religions, also used catacombs for burials.

Around the 2nd century AD, the population of Rome was growing quickly and there was a lack of usable land within the city. There was also an ancient Roman law that forbade burials within the city, so all places of burial including catacombs were outside the city walls. The first catacombs on a large scale were dug starting in the 2nd century AD and were used through the first half of the 5th century.

There are hundreds of miles of catacombs throughout Rome either within the city center of in the "suburbs."

Here are a few of the more famous of the Rome Catacombs:

Catacombs of San Sebastian - These are Rome's oldest catacombs. The remains of St. Sebastian (one of Rome's greatest martyrs) are interred here. These catacombs are 12 kilometers (7.5 miles) long.

Catacombs of San Callisto - This is not the oldest of the catacombs, but it is the largest. The catacombs of San Callisto are named after Deacon St. Callixtus. Among the roughly 500,000 Christians buried there, there are many of Rome's most famous martyrs and 16 early popes. The Papal Tombs are very impressive and very popular, drawing in the crowds. The catacombs of San Callisto are 20 kilometers (12.4 miles) long.

Catacombs of Priscilla - Priscilla is known as the "queen of the catacombs" because there are so many martyrs buried here. Priscilla was a Roman noblewoman who allowed the church to use her vast land for burials.

Catacombs of Domitilla - This is one of the oldest and largest of the catacombs of Rome. There are over 150,000 people buried here. The catacombs stretch over 17 kilometers (10.5 miles).

Catacombs of Sant'Agnese - Sant'Agnese was a martyr for the Christian faith. She is buried in these catacombs that now bear her name.

Catacombs of Praetextatus - Located along the Appian Way, these catacombs date back to the 2nd century. The tunnels of this set of catacombs are famous for artwork and for the burial of various Christian martyrs. In one of the oldest sections of the catacombs is a depiction of Christ being crowned with the crown of thorns.

Catacombs of San Pancrazio - This catacomb is under the San Pancrazio Basilica. The body of the young martyr Saint Pancras (Pancratius) is buried in this set of catacombs.

Visiting the Catacombs of Rome may not be for everyone, but they are a part of the history of Rome. In addition to places of burials in the catacombs, you will see frescos (painted murals done on freshly laid line plaster) and paintings or other artwork.

Interesting Facts about the Catacombs of Rome

- A lot of children died during the early centuries. There are special burial places crested just for children in the catacombs.

- In addition to being the final resting place to thousands of people, the Catacombs of Rome is an amazing underground art gallery. There are paintings and etchings along the walls that help to shed light on the life of Christians in pagan Rome.

- The Catacomb of Priscilla holds the remains of two popes, Pope Marcellinus (296-304 AD) and Pope Marcellus I (308-309 AD).

Chapter 13

National Museum of Rome

The National Museum of Rome (Archaeological Museum of Rome) is actually a collection of four separate museums located in different areas of the city of Rome. The museum was founded in 1889 and inaugurated in 1890 as a museum to collect and exhibit archaeological materials from excavations after Rome was united with the Kingdom of Italy. The history of the museum then started with the archaeological collections of the Kircherian Museum. In 1901, more museums and collections were added to the national museum. More changes took place from 1911-1930. In 1990, the museum was totally renovated, dividing the collections into the current four museums. The four museums are the Baths of Diocletian, the Palazzo Altemps, the Crypta Balbi, and the Palazzo Massimo alle Terme.

Palazzo Massimo alle Terme

The building where this museum is housed is a palace that was built between 1883 and 1887. The Palazzo Massimo holds one of the best archaeological and classical art collections in the world!

National Museum of Rome - Palazzo Massimo alle Terme

Thermal Baths of Diocletian

The baths were built between 292 AD and 306 AD. Later in the 16th century, a monastery and church complex became a part of the baths. On the tour, you can see part of the grounds of the largest thermal baths in Roman period. The main cloister was designed and built by

Michelangelo. The collections housed there are mainly bronze and marble statues.

National Museum of Rome - Baths of Diocletian

Crypta Balbi

The Crypta Balbi is an exhibit of Rome from the 5th century AD and early Middle Ages. It is housed in the building that used to be the theater of Balbus.

Palazzo Altemps

Palazzo Altemps is fairly close to Piazza Navona. This museum contains ancient sculptures from Roman nobility. This palace was named for Cardinal Marcus Sitticus Altemps who owned this building.

National Museum of Rome - Palazzo Altemps

Fun Facts about the National Museum of Rome

- Built by Emperor Diocletian in 305 AD, the Baths of Diocletian were the biggest thermal complex in Ancient Rome. They had a capacity for more than 3,000 people.

- Originally consisting of a theater, a four-story block, and a courtyard, the Crypta Balbi was built between 19 and 13 BC for Lucius Cornelius Balbus.

- A Renaissance building built between 1883 and 1887, Palazzo Massimo has one of the best archaeological collections in the world.

- Palazzo Altemps houses an important collection of Greek and Roman sculptures belonging to families of the Roman nobility of the 16th and 17th centuries.

Chapter 14

Ara Pacis (Altar of Peace)

More commonly known as Ara Pacis, the Ara Pacis Augustae (Altar of Augustan Peace) is an altar dedicated to Pax, the Roman goddess of peace. It was built in 13 BC to celebrate Augustus' (Caesar Augustus - the first Roman Emperor reigning 27 BC to 14 AD) return from his campaigns in Gaul and Spain. The Altar of Peace is a marble structure which previously stood on the Campus Martius, a publicly owned area of Rome about 2 square kilometers (0.77 square miles) in size.

The altar's original location was in the flood plain of the Tiber River. It was gradually buried in 4 meters (13 feet) mud and silt. It remained in that location until it was reassembled in its current museum in 1938. The altar is designed as a traditional (for ancient Rome) open-air altar with openings on the eastern and western ends.

The entire structure is delicately sculpted in marble. The designs on the altar show the family of Augustus and different depictions of the life and times of the era.

The Altar of Peace

Fun Facts about the Ara Pacis

- The 3-meter (9.84 feet) altar is set on a pedestal that is 7 meters (22.97 feet) tall in an open-air structure with four walls that are over 11 meters (36.1 feet) tall. The pedestal is decorated with priests and sacrificial animals.

- The material used to create the Ara Pacis (Altar of Peace) is called Luna marble.

- Before the altar was put back together and

displayed in the Museum of the Ara Pacis, various fragments of the altar were found in different museums around Europe.

Chapter 15

Vatican Museums

To begin this section, let's talk a little about Vatican City. An independent city-state and enclave, Vatican City is also simply called the Vatican. It has been fully independent (as its own country) from Italy since 1929 as a part of the Lateran Treaty. The Lateran Treaty was an agreement between the Kingdom of Italy and the Holy See (the authority of the Pope as the Bishop of Rome) that settled papal sovereignty over Vatican City and Italy's sovereignty over the former papal states (a group of territories along the Italy peninsula which were previously under the sovereign rule of the pope). Vatican City is the home of Roman Catholicism, the world's most popular religion, and it is the smallest country in the world. On top of that, more than 6 million people visit Vatican City every year!

Vatican City has public museums called the Vatican Museums. The museums include 24 galleries including the Sistine Chapel and St. Peter's Basilica. The museums contain close to 70,000 works of art (20,000 are on display). Included in the works are many renowned Roman sculptures and some of the most important Renaissance art (sculptures, paintings, and decorative arts from the Renaissance period – around 1400 AD) found anywhere.

Vatican Museums

The Vatican Museums are one of the most visited art museums in the world! The beginnings of the museums can be traced back to 1506 when the sculpture called *Laocoon and His Sons* was discovered in a vineyard near the basilica of Santa Maria Maggiore. Pope Julius II purchased the sculpture from the vineyard owner and placed it on public display in the Vatican.

Laocoon and His Sons sculpture

Highlights of the Vatican Museums in addition to the sculpture of *Laocoon and His Sons* include:

- The red marble papal throne

- The Raphael Rooms, displaying many works by Raphael

- The Niccoline Chapel, noted for fresco paintings by Fra Angelico (1447-1451)

- The Sistine Chapel including the ceiling painted by Michelangelo

Fun Facts about Vatican City and the Vatican Museums

- Some people have estimated that if you took one minute to look at each painting in the Vatican Museums, it would take you 4 years to completely see all of the paintings in the museums.

- Vatican City does not have an official language. People there speak English, French, Italian, German, and Spanish.

- Vatican City has the smallest population of any country in the world with only about 1000 people calling it home.

- If you joined all of the Vatican Museums' rooms together in a line, it would extend for 9 miles.

Chapter 16

Sistine Chapel

The Sistine Chapel is a part of the Vatican Museums. It is a major attraction for tourists to Vatican City, not only because of the magnificent ceiling painting by Michelangelo and the other major paintings throughout but because it is the location of the papal conclaves (the election of a Pope by the College of Cardinals).

From the outside, the Sistine Chapel is rather non-descript. It is a rectangular building with six arched windows on each of the two main sides. The exterior of the chapel is not decorated with architectural details like most Italian churches. Its entrance is through rooms internal to the Papal Palace, and its exterior can only be seen from windows of the surrounding buildings. The building itself has three stories: a basement, the chapel, and a wardroom for guards. The third story has a roofed gangway which is supported by an arcade (a series of arches that are strengthened by the push that each arch exerts on the other) that is sloped from the building.

Sistine Chapel exterior

Inside the chapel, the design consists of a barrel-vaulted ceiling (a curved ceiling creating a single continuous archway). Painted by Michelangelo between 1508 and 1512, the Sistine Chapel ceiling is a foundation of High Renaissance art. The paintings of the ceiling alone brings many visitors each year.

Fun Facts about the Sistine Chapel

- Michelangelo did not really want to work on the Sistine Chapel paintings. He considered himself more of a sculptor than a painter.

- Before Michelangelo started work on painting the chapel ceiling, it had been painted with a blue night sky with golden stars by the Umbrian artist Piero Matteo d'Amelia.

- Pictures of Michelangelo painting the Sistine Chapel show him and his assistants lying down. He actually painted the Sistine Chapel in a standing position.

- Michelangelo designed his own scaffolding system which attached to the wall.

Chapter 17

St. Peter's Basilica

Saint Peter's Basilica is also known by its proper name Papal Basilica of Saint Peter in the Vatican. St. Peter's is one of the four Major Basilicas in Rome. The other three Major Basilicas in Rome are St. John Lateran, St. Mary Major (Santa Maria Maggiore), and St. Paul's outside the Walls. One of the largest churches in Christendom, the basilica is the most prominent building in Vatican City, covering 5.7 acres.

St. Peter's Square is in front of the basilica. The square is a court in two sections both surrounded by tall colonnades (a row of columns supporting a roof or support). The colonnade in St. Peter's square encloses a wide-open space that is elliptical in shape.

Panoramic view of St. Peter's Square

St. Peter's Square from St. Peter's Basilica

The dome of the basilica is 136.57 meters (448.1 feet) high from the floor to the external cross on the top. It is one of the most impressive parts of this basilica. Michelangelo had a part in the design of the dome. The design was continued by Giacomo Della Porta and completed in 1614 by Carlo Maderno. St. Peter's dome inspired many other cathedrals – the capitol building in Washington DC and St. Paul's Cathedral in London are just two examples.

The name of the basilica comes from one of Jesus' twelve disciples, Saint Peter. Saint Peter is believed to be one of the founders of the Roman Catholic Church. Peter was executed in Rome and is buried where the basilica stands.

Fun Facts about St. Peter's Basilica

- St. Peter's Basilica is the final resting place of 91 popes.

- There are sculptures of 140 various saints atop the colonnade in the square. The sculptures were completed by various artists between 1662-1703.

- Although still being discussed, the reason why the altar of the current St. Peter's was built where it is was because it is thought that St. Peter's remains are buried directly under the altar.

- The Basilica has a Holy Door that is only opened during holy years such as jubilee.

Chapter 18

Rome Bike Tours

Bike tours can be one sure way of seeing the most sites of Rome in the least amount of time and get some exercise while enjoying the views! Many of the bike tours in Rome are via e-bikes (electric bikes) that help you navigate hills with ease. But whether by regular bike or e-bikes, your tour guide will make the trip memorable!

Here are a few companies that offer bike tours in Rome:

Top Bike Rental and Tours

Top Bike offers guided tours by e-bike and also bike rentals. The company offers a unique way to see Rome with their 4-hour City Center Highlights tour. If you are looking for more, they also have a Rome in One Day tour that includes a lunch at a local trattoria. Other options include a 6 hour off the beaten path tour.

Fat Tire Bike Tours

Fat Tire Bike Tours offers a day tour that gives a great overview of the top attractions in Rome and a night tour option that tours the popular Trastevere neighborhood. Fat Tire also offers a private bike tour option offering a little more time for questions and explanations at the various stops along the way.

Roma Star Bike

Roma Star offers a variety of e-bike tours throughout the city. They offer an early morning (8 am in the summer months) bike tour which is a great option to beat the heat and the crowds. Additionally, Roma Star offers a night tour close to sunset to allow a different view of the history of Rome. Roma Star also offers a couple of tours along the Appian Way.

Chapter 19

Rome Walking Tours

Walking is a great way to explore Rome. The city is a very busy place as it is a bustling, modern, working city, so walking is one of the best ways to get from one place to another. Walking with a tour guide who can share tips and history just makes it even more fun!

Here are some tour companies that offer walking tours of Rome:

Walks of Italy

Walks of Italy started out with two guides giving great tours of the Rome Colosseum and has just grown and grown from there – all over Italy. They offer a variety of tours including several great tours of the colosseum as well as food tours (fine food and street food). Walks of

Italy even offers day trips. Their motto is *Don't Take Just Any Tour. Take Walks.*

City Wonders

City Wonders started touring in 2004 with a tour called the *Dark Heart of Rome.* They still pride themselves on offering the Original Rome Crypts and Catacombs tour. City Tours offers tours of just about every attraction in Rome including the Colosseum and the Vatican / St. Peter's Basilica, but they also offer full day trip tours of surrounding areas.

LivItaly Tours

Don't just visit Italy. Live It! is the motto at LivItaly Tours. From full-day Rome walking tours to private experiences at the Colosseum, you will find many tours here. They have one of the most extensive tour offerings that is available anywhere.

With Locals

With Locals offers 100% private walking tours of Rome. Imagine a walk with a photographer, personal shopping with a Vouge Journalist, a family treasure hunt at the Vatican Museums, Secret Rome (The Dark Side), or Seeing Rome as a Gladiator. These are just some of the interesting tours available.

I hope you enjoyed your trip to Rome! I have a fun puzzle and coloring page download to go along with the book. This fun addition is free to download here:

https://kid-friendly-family-vacations.com/romefun

Please consider adding a review to help other readers learn more about Rome whether traveling or learning from home. Thanks!

https://kid-friendly-family-vacations.com/review-rome

Also By Teresa Mills and Kid Friendly Family Vacations

Hey Kids! Let's Visit Washington DC
Hey Kids! Let's Visit A Cruise Ship
Hey Kids! Let's Visit New York City
Hey Kids! Let's Visit London England
Hey Kids! Let's Visit San Francisco
Hey Kids! Let's Visit Savannah Georgia
Hey Kids! Let's Visit Paris France
Hey Kids! Let's Visit Charleston South Carolina
Hey Kids! Let's Visit Chicago
Hey Kids! Let's Visit Rome Italy
Hey Kids! Let's Visit Boston
Hey Kids! Let's Visit Philadelphia
Hey Kids! Let's Visit San Diego
Hey Kids! Let's Visit Seattle
Hey Kids! Let's Visit Seoul South Korea
Hey Kids! Let's Visit Atlanta
Hey Kids! Let's Visit Dublin Ireland

More from Kid Friendly Family Vacations

BOOKS

Books to help build your kids / grandkids life experiences through travel and learning
https://kid-friendly-family-vacations.com/books

COLORING AND ACTIVITY PAGKAGES

Coloring pages, activity books, printable travel journals, and more in our Etsy shop
https://kid-friendly-family-vacations.com/etsy

RESOURCES FOR TEACHERS

Resources for teachers on Teachers Pay Teachers
https://kid-friendly-family-vacations.com/tpt

It is our mission to help you build your children's and grand-children's life experiences through travel. Not just traveling with your kids... building their Life Experiences"! Join our community here:
https://kid-friendly-family-vacations.com/join

Acknowledgements

Proofreading / Editing

Katie Erickson – KatieEricksonEditing.com

Cover Photos

The Colosseum – © artjazz / depositphotos.com

The Roman Forum – © sborisov / depositphotos.com

Trevi Fountain – © karambol / depositphotos.com

Arch of Constantine – © tan4ikk / depositphotos.com

Photos in Book

The Pantheon – © lakov / depositphotos.com
The Colosseum (vertical) – © tank_bmb / depositphotos.com

The Colosseum – interior – © personal vacation photo
Capitoline Hill – © CAHKT / depositphotos.com

Santa Maria Maggiore – © Leonid_Adronov / depositphotos.com

Palatine Hill - House of Augustus – © phillyo77 / depositphotos.com

Palatine Hill – Domitian's Hippodrome – © ramana16.gmail.com / depositphotos.com

The Roman Forum – © sborisov / depositphotos.com

Arch of Constantine – © tan4ikk / depositphotos.com

Galleria Borghese – © karambol / depositphotos.com

Trevi Fountain – © karambol / depositphotos.com

Piazza Navona – © sborisov / depositphotos.com

Spanish Steps – © sborisov / depositphotos.com

National Museum of Rome – Baths of Diocletian – © mauriziobiso_1 / depositphotos.com

National Museum of Rome – Palazzo Altemps – © jorumba75 / depositphotos.com

National Museum of Rome – Palazzo Massimo – © paanna /depositphotos.com Ara Pacis – © toucanet / depositphotos.com

Vatican Museums – © Antartis / depositphotos.com

Vatican Museums - Lacooon and his sons – © DimitarMitev / depositphotos.com

Sistine Chapel – © Yarr / depositphotos.com

St. Peters Basilica - panorama – © MadrugadaVerde / depositphotos.com

St. Peter's Square – © Phillyo77 / depositphotos.com

About the Author

Teresa Mills is the bestselling author of the "Hey Kids! Let's Visit..." Book Series for Kids! Teresa's goal through her books and website is to help parents / grandparents who want to build the life experiences of their children / grandchildren through travel and learning activities.

She is an active mother and Mimi. She and her family love traveling in the USA, and internationally too! They love exploring new places, eating cool foods, and having yet another adventure as a family! With the Mills, it's all about traveling as family.

In addition to traveling, Teresa enjoys reading, hiking, biking, and helping others.

Join in the fun at

kid-friendly-family-vacations.com

Made in the USA
Monee, IL
20 February 2025

12663475R00056